Someday You'll Write

Also by Elizabeth Yates

ELIZABETH YATES

Someday You'll Write

E. P. DUTTON & CO., INC., NEW YORK

Published simultaneously in Canada by
Clarke, Irwin & Company Limited, Toronto and Vancouver

Library of Congress Catalog Card Number: 62-14706

ACKNOWLEDGMENTS
The author wishes to thank Harper & Row, publishers of
Charlotte's Web by E. B. White, and Frederick Warne & Co., Inc.,
publishers of *The Tale of Tom Kitten* by Beatrix Potter,
for permission to quote from those two books.

> Get thy tools ready,
> God will find the work.
> —BROWNING

ONE day, Joyce asked me for a book on writing. I was not sure that I knew what she meant, so she explained that she wanted to know how books were written and how a person got to be a writer.

She has often asked me for particular books, and generally I've been able to find them, but this request was not an easy one to satisfy. Our library had nothing, so I went further afield and made inquiries of friends, librarians, even publishers. But there was no such book to be found. Of course, there were a number of books on the techniques of writing, the development of literary skills, the making of books, but these were all written for grown-ups, and would be waiting for Joyce in the years ahead. What she wanted to read now, at the age of eleven-going-on-twelve, had not yet been written. I told her that we would have to write such a book together, and asked her to bring me a list of what she would like to find in the book.

Quite unintentionally, Joyce had stumbled on Rule

5

Number One in writing, which is: If an idea comes to you that there should be something written on a particular subject, and you find that there is nothing, it may be up to you to do it. Now, whenever Joyce and I are together she exemplifies Rule Number Two, and always has a big pad and a sharp pencil at hand. She wants to be a writer someday. I wanted to be a writer before I knew how to read. As the years went on, some people told me that it was hard work and others that I would get over it and want to be something else. But I didn't. The ability to write is a long time growing. Joyce realizes this, and wants to begin now.

At the top of her list she wrote *What I'd Like to Find in the Book.* The chapters that follow are my way of answering her.

CONTENTS

Someday You'll Write

At the Beginning

You say that you want to be a writer someday, that you dream of being one; but you know, as well as I do, that we cannot dream ourselves into being anything. We can, though, through work and acceptance of the discipline, shape ourselves into being what we want to be. In the Middle Ages young boys were apprenticed to master craftsmen for a period of years, seven generally, to learn their skills. You might think thus of these immediate years during which you will be acquiring skills for later work. Your apprenticeship, however, will not be to a single master, but to the great masters of English prose whose words have moved and enriched and delighted people for a very long time.

You say that you like to read. That goes hand in hand with your desire to write, and will help you more than anything else.

An apprentice must learn first of all how to use well the tools of his trade, and books will be one of your tools—books that have stood through the years, books that stretch your mind and make you reach high above yourself, and stir you deep within yourself, books that give you gay and honest enjoyment of the world in which you are a part.

What books do you like best to read? Take one of them and read it again, not rushing along with the story to see what happens, but savoring it. It is a good book, of that you are sure. But just why is it good? Where did your interest quicken? What happened to make you feel you were an actual part of the story? With what character did you find you were identifying yourself, and why? At the end, perhaps there were tears in your eyes, perhaps you were smiling—but was it so satisfying that whatever happened you felt right about it? Did you feel as you put the book back on the shelf that you would go on living with it for a long time, that something of it had become yours forever?

How was it that you felt all this, and perhaps much more? If you can begin to discover some of the reasons, you will be laying a sound foundation for your own approach to writing. It is not easy, this endeavor to reduce a book to its structure. It might be compared to reducing a house that now is being lived in comfortably to the architect's drawing before the house was built. To study the plan will reveal much that is taken for granted in the finished structure.

Read this way with a particular book and it will quicken your sense of it as a story; it will also sharpen your eye for the shape of a sentence, the content of a paragraph. Your inner ear will begin to respond to the sound of the words and the way they are used in relation to each other. Their aptness and the way they conveyed beauty and spoke truth were all part of what held you to the book.

Notice particular words, perhaps new to you or new in their context, and add them to your own vocabulary. Here, again, are tools, and the sensitive craftsman will care for words as for any valued piece of equipment. Try your newly acquired words in different combinations; experiment with them as an artist does with colors. Words serve their purpose when well employed. This is done when their meaning is clearly understood. One book that should be within your easy reach is the dictionary. Add to your store of words constantly, but no faster than you can master their meaning.

A book is the result of long thinking and much hard work. It is carefully constructed, though this will not be in the least apparent when it is finished. In fact, as you are discovering with your reading, it may prove difficult to find the structure on which the book is built. But, if you can accept this kind of analysis as

part of your discipline as an apprentice, you will have
made a strong start. Every skill imposes its own discipline. That word may seem a hard one, but it is
rewarding. See how the dictionary defines it and how
it applies to your desire to be a writer. "Discipline:
training or experience that corrects, molds, strengthens, or perfects" (Webster).

The reading of books, the gradual mastery of words
are general tools. Your own highly personal ones are
the jottings you make in your notebook. Keep a notebook always near—in your pocket during the day, on
the table by your bed at night. You never know when
you may see something unusual or provoking or beautiful, and if you jot it down you can think more about
it later on. Use your notebook as an artist does a
sketchbook, drawing something in a few words that
can be elaborated on with more time.

You may hear an exchange of conversation on a
street corner that would fit well into a story. You may
catch the curious sound of an unfamiliar word whose
meaning you want to look up. There will be times—
perhaps while you are walking in the woods or watch-
ing a sunset—when you will want to dash down a
description right on the spot rather than wait until
you get home. Impressions should be caught as close
to the time of seeing, hearing, feeling, discovering as
possible, so the emotion can be captured with the

image. Ideas may come to you out of the blue and in the oddest moments, so jot them down for future exploration. This is all raw material for writing, and your notebooks can be a rich storehouse from which you may draw at will.

You ask if you should use a typewriter. Of course you should learn to use one, as it, too, in its way and its time, is a tool; but first, in the early days of your apprenticeship, use well the ancient tools. Fingers curling around a pencil can often help the mind to embrace an idea; the pencil shaping words can often aid the shaping of thoughts.

You ask where to write and when. If I say in a quiet place with a span of undisturbed time, I am stating ideal working conditions. Train yourself to write anywhere, at any time, for you will often have to do just that. And write something every day. Constant practice is requisite for a writer, as it is for a pianist or a tightrope walker. Write letters. Keep a diary. Compose poems. Draw on the ideas in your notebooks. Your fingers will clasp a pencil as they do a friend's hand, and your thoughts will flow onto a piece of paper as they do in conversation, if you give them the chance. Write, not only when an idea grips you or you are in the mood, but because you are developing a skill and you want to keep yourself in training.

You have read about inspiration, and you will read more, but inspiration has two aspects—one may be the wild horse that, when mounted, gallops off to high and marvelous places or races headlong into a treacherous marsh; the other aspect is of the well-trained steed that, when mounted, responds to the rider's signals and canters off to high and marvelous places or wherever the rider wants him to go. The difference is all in the control. If an idea seizes you—and that is a form of inspiration for the writer—see how you can make it serve your purpose at the time, and decide where you want to go with it.

Write whether you feel like it or not, whether you really want to or not, but write every day practice pieces for your own eye that you will freely discard. Set aside a period of time for your writing. Your friends may, at first, try to lure you away; but they will soon begin to respect your determination, even though they think you a little odd. Writing never appears to be work, or serious, except to the writer, and you might just as well get used to that attitude now and come to terms with it.

A table with enough space for you to write with ease is better than a desk, for a desk often has on it things that distract attention. On your table should be the immediate tools of your trade—a big pad, several pencils, and a dictionary. This is the place where you have come to write down in some kind of form what you have been thinking about. If you have thought carefully and clearly, the chances are that when you pick up your pencil the words will flow almost as if the lead within the wood had an electric quality that has been set in motion by the impulses in your brain. If you have not thought through your idea, the chances are that doodles rather than words may fill your page.

Six hundred years ago, Chaucer's "deere maister," Geoffrey de Vinsauf, said: "If one has a house to build, the impetuous hand does not rush to the act; the innermost line of the heart measures the work in advance, and the inner man prescribes a course according to the established plan; the hand of the mind fashions the whole before that of the body. . . . When a plan has arranged the subject in the secret place of the mind, poetry will come to clothe the matter with words."

However, thinking conditions are not always ideal, just as working conditions are not. If this is so, and the writing does not come easily and the paper looks very blank, you can always "play a few scales," as it were (as your friend may be doing as she practices the piano next door). You can write a letter to yourself. After the first paragraph or two it may swing into being the story you have been thinking about. It may begin to take on a life of its own. It may become something quite different from what you had in mind. Let it, for any story has its own life to live. The words that cover the page surprise you, for you intended to do a certain something and now you are doing something else. And yet these are words that you find you want to set down, and you feel that if you don't they may be lost forever.

When this happens, write swiftly to catch the flow from the newly discovered spring within you. Don't stop to reach for the right word or to correct your grammar; all that can be done later. This, that you are experiencing, is sheer creativity. It is what makes the act of writing a thrilling adventure.

Bring to completion the stint you set yourself, whether it is a whole story, an episode in a story, a page of conversation, or a descriptive paragraph. Finish it before you go on to something else. All kinds of excuses keep coming up not to finish something started but to begin something else. There is only one word for this, and it is "temptation." Learn in your apprentice days to run these temptations to ground as you would any other. Unfinished work is discouraging. It is a downward drag from the high course you have set. To keep beginning again, though it may be stimulating, is never satisfying. Each finished stint, be it only a paragraph that you have completed to your own satisfaction, is a minor triumph—a single feather in the pair of lifting wings that will bear you onward.

This is hard: to keep at something until it pleases you. You are not only the creator but the critic, too, and your work will have to please you before it can possibly please anyone else. To finish what you have begun requires strength of mind, as well as purpose and a sense of time that have nothing to do with clock or calendar. It is never lack of time that keeps people from accomplishment, but rather a lack of directed energy, of order, of the ability to assemble ideas and put them to use. If your heart is really set on what you are doing, you will find the time and the place, and the persistence within your own self to do it.

These tools about which we have been talking are all tangible and real, but there are invisible tools, too, that are fully as important as your notebook, pad and pencil, and your wide and wonderful reading. They are three, and they will be familiar to you because they are in the old fairy tales—the cloak of invisibility, the pair of magic shoes, and the little stone that has the power to turn all it touches into gold. Perhaps you had never thought of them as being part of a writer's equipment, but let me show you how this can be so.

The cloak that makes its wearer invisible at times is something that a writer seems to be born with. You may not have been aware of this, but you will learn of the cloak the more you use it. Sometimes it is put on intentionally; sometimes it puts itself on, and then the wearer must act accordingly. This happens to me often, like the day when I stood at the counter in a grocery store waiting to make my purchases. When the clerk was free, I started to say what I wanted, when to my amazement he turned his attention to a customer who had just appeared and asked her what she would like. I opened my mouth to speak because, after all, she had only just come in and I had been standing there for several minutes; but I caught myself just in time and realized that I had on my cloak of invisibility.

Another five minutes passed before the clerk finished with two other customers; then he greeted me and said: "I didn't see you come in. What can I do for you?" I told him, but I didn't say that I had been waiting, for during the time of invisibility such a conversation I had heard! It consisted not only of words, but of attitudes and points of view, two, in fact, that were revealing and valuable. It reminded me of what Uncle Zed Canfield said to his niece Dorothy when she was a little girl: "If you want to learn something about a man or a woman, Dolly, and the town they live in, don't ask them direct questions. Listen while they think they are talking about something else."

An invisible cloak permits one to do a great deal of

listening and observing in all kinds of places. And to learn to listen, not with the ears only but with the eyes and heart, is very important for a writer. Don't be disturbed if you find you have your cloak on unintentionally. Look for the reason. There always is one. And wear your cloak often. The only thing that can ever wear it out is disuse.

Magic shoes can be used to good advantage with the cloak, but they perform well under all conditions. People think a writer is confined to his desk, but they do not know how far and deep he travels, not only to other places but also into other lives. Keats said: "If a sparrow comes before my window, I take part in its existence and pick about in the gravel." Hans Andersen wore his magic shoes often, as Thumbelina, the Little Mermaid, and a host of his characters testify. Put on your magic shoes; note how well they fit and how comfortable they are; then step into another period of time, another environment, wriggle down inside another's skin. There is no height that the shoes cannot climb over, no depth they cannot fathom, no horizon they cannot cross. Everything is within their reach—the farthest country, the nearest chipmunk hole.

The third piece of magic, the stone, is small and round and ordinary. It looks like a hundred others on a road or a beach; but it looks like the others only to those who have not developed eyes to see its value. It is so close that you may stub your toe on it or you may even kick it out of the way. Then, one day, you pick it up and begin to handle it. Your eyes open to the fact that this ordinary stone is no ordinary thing. It stands for an experience you have had, or call it an idea that teases your mind. You have discredited it because it seems insignificant and you doubt whether it is really any good. Then you begin to see that within the idea, or the experience, is a story. It is there if you can go far enough into it to find its wonder and its truth. You sense a kind of glory creeping around the edges of your mind. It is as if all your random thoughts were being brought into sharp focus. The little stone has, indeed, the capacity to turn all to gold if it is handled rightly. With the greatest care you put the stone in your pocket, tuck the idea away in your mind to think about at leisure.

Others will see your tangible tools, but no one will ever know anything about your invisible ones until you have put them to use. They are valuable equipment. Living in your imagination, and fed by it, they are indestructible. But magic has always had a way of following certain rules. In the old fairy tales it would never work for the hesitant or the fearful, but it would do great things for the bold and the warm-hearted. It can do nothing of itself, but coupled with

hard work, ingenuity, and love it can break any spell
or, for the writer, create a binding spell of words.

Those are the qualities you will need to embrace—
hard work, ingenuity, love. The last is the key that
opens every door. When the princess loved the ugly
frog enough to kiss him, he became a prince before
her eyes; when Beauty loved the beast enough, he
turned into his true self. When a writer cares enough
to work long and hard and put all that he is into his
work, something wonderful is bound to happen.

How to Select a Subject

You ask how to select a subject, and this is good, for on your choice depends the excitement you will have in developing it. But what if I should say to you that often the writer does not select a subject so much as the subject select the writer?

Subjects are all about us. They may be in a chance remark heard in a crowded bus, in an item read in a newspaper, in something seen, like the first robin or a rainbow spanning the sky. Everything has a story to tell, but the story told to one person is different from that told to another. Often the best subjects are found in our everyday lives, but they go unrealized because they are so near. Even a mountain on the horizon can go unseen by some people for the simple reason that it is always there.

Here are six subjects:

The Birthday Present
A Boy Takes His Pet Rabbit to a Fair

The Big Storm
A Girl—or a Boy—Walks Home from School
My Favorite Tree
Christmas at Grandmother's

About one of them you may want to write a story—
a story, remember, not an essay or a piece of biography, but a story because right now you and I are
talking about something that is made up. Fiction. It
will start from an experience or a memory, something
that you can link to yourself and to which you can
respond; but your imagination working on it will
create something else that is new and real. A rich and
rewarding thing it is to tell a story, and it is one of
the most ancient of the arts. It reaches back to the
time when a group of people sat by a fire in a cave
with shadows flickering on the walls and listened to
one of their number. Outside, there might have been
danger and cold; beyond a known area there might
have been unknown terrors; but within there were
warmth, comfort, security—and more than those three
—wonder, as the listeners were spellbound by the
weaving of words. From earliest days the prime purpose of a story has been to entertain, and that will
be your purpose, too, when you decide on the subject that will give scope to your imagination.

Think about those six subjects, and see if one of

them allures you a little more than the others. That *if* is important, for you will have to be really caught up by the possibilities in an idea before you can find your way with it. As an exercise in writing—the mechanics of writing, that is—you could probably take any one of the six and, if you thought about it enough, do a reasonably good paper.

What was the present that meant most to you on your last birthday?

You've never kept rabbits, but you may know a boy who keeps them and you might do an interview with him.

Remember that big storm last winter and how the town was crippled for twenty-four hours?

It might not seem exciting to write about a tree, but wait—what if you got right inside the tree and thought of what it is like to be a hemlock or an apple or an oak that has known three hundred years pass by it?

And you do spend Christmas at your grandmother's, don't you?

Yes, of course, you could write about any one of them, dealing with the facts and making a direct and careful presentation. You could put your hand on the required information and do something that would be entirely creditable. Once written, you could check it for spelling and grammar, work over it a bit more, recopy it as if it were a school composition. If it were, and if you turned it in, the likelihood is that you would get a good mark. All the same, not one of those five subjects mentioned and about which you might have written set your imagination on fire. With them your hand would not race across the page, nor would the words come alive as the idea took life from you. I wonder why. They are all within your range, but not one of them touched you.

Based on experience or knowledge, as writing is, the spark that is needed is the story quality in the subject, and that must come from your inmost self. Only the sense of a story within an idea will touch off a fire of creativity. But there is one subject that teases your imagination, and it is *A Girl—or a Boy—Walks Home from School*. This, then, is the start: where you are, with what you know. Now you can go on to what you feel deeply about.

For the sake of a story, let us say that one day you walk home from school and everything is quite as usual. Your arms are filled with books, your thoughts are far ahead of you. Glancing down, your eye is caught by the small flash of something shining in the gutter. You bend down to see what it is and you pick up a little silver locket, or, if you are writing from the boy's angle, a pocket watch. So far, this is what might happen on almost any day, but from now on it be comes a story. Your imagination is free to do what it will.

You rub the locket or the watch against your sleeve to clean it. It must have lain there some time, for it is dirty and scratched with grit from the street, but it can still shine. It looks old. You wonder who could have lost it and how you can find the owner. You turn it in your hands and discover that it has initials engraved on it. *J. T.* You stare. Those are your initials, but this *J. T.* is not you.

And now your imagination begins to race. Just as the small shining in the gutter gave back light to the sun, so an ordinary event like walking home from school glows with extraordinary possibilities. Did you select the subject or did it you? Whatever happened, it has filled your mind and set you thinking as you start to work out a plot, decide on the people involved, determine their various adventures. You can hardly wait to get home to your quiet corner, to go on thinking with a pencil held between your fingers and a pad under your hand. Thoreau, who has much to say to writers, puts it this way: "It is in vain to write on chosen themes. We must wait till they have kindled a flame in our minds. The theme seeks me, not I it."

A story within an everyday event has struck a spark within you, and with all your heart you long to write it in the most effective way possible with the most beautiful language you can command, but you know that you must think it through first. If one of your school friends caught up with you and asked you what you were thinking about, you would probably answer, "Nothing," and let it go at that. Your writer's instinct has come to your aid. If you tell the story now in this early stage, you may find there is nothing left to write later on.

Your mind has become like a question box—who? what? when? To find the answers stretches your curiosity. Why? How? Where? Your imagination begins to supply the answers, but each one will have to be weighed against the total weight of the story. The nub of it all is to find the owner of the treasure. Around and around that your thinking revolves. It might be— and you think of someone you know in school with the initials *J. T.*, but he is a boy, and what would a boy be doing with a locket? It might be—and you think of a crotchety old woman who lives in an ancient house on a high and lonely hill a mile outside town. Perhaps it belongs to her.

One thought follows another; one character seems to demand another. You begin to feel like a spider sitting in the center of a web of intermingling relationships. Out of yourself you have spun the web, out of the thoughts and feelings you have held, the sights and sounds you have known. So much that you have been thinking about lately comes into focus. Now, something you very much want to say appears to be the strongest thread in the web, the web that holds all the relationships together. You work from the inside out with a center that is well defined and a circumference that is expandable.

Don't be surprised if your thoughts do not soon resolve themselves into an orderly pattern. It takes time for an idea to achieve its own life; it will take a great deal of time for you to feel your way into that life. But you know now that you will have to make a plan, even before you start to write, so you can keep clear before you what it is you want to say and have some sense of the direction in which you want to go. If you make such a plan and jot down in your notebook the thoughts that have been pouring into your mind, you will have the story-idea in a safe place.

An idea will do a good deal of developing on its own. Like a seed, it has its power of growing within it. You are the good soil that will give the idea a place to root and take hold. All that gives richness to your mind—school, friends, books, interests—will add richness to the idea that has found lodgment in you and that makes of you only one demand: that you write it in your own way.

So you make an outline, not a mold but a pattern that is loose and flexible. Within it you determine how

you want to start and you set down the ending that
you want to achieve. List your chief characters, the
major episodes, the setting, and the basic underlying
idea; then write a brief paragraph to yourself on what
you want the story to be and do. Once you begin to
write, all this may change. As the story gains its own
life it may do something quite different, but you will
be starting with the reins held lightly in your hands
and you will be in no danger of getting lost.

A cook following a recipe may add a little more
sugar here, a little less milk there, because it will suit
her particular purpose. Carpenters following a blue-
print for a house can, with the owner's consent, make
alterations to meet changing needs, but the framework
is there and within it the house comes into being. So
within your outline the story you have set yourself to
tell will grow. If the story begins to run away with
you as you write, reread that brief paragraph you wrote
about it and see if you want it to go the way it is
going or if you prefer to bring it back to your original
intent.

Sometimes, when you write, the words come from
the page as if they were written there in invisible ink
and the warmth of the hand on the page made them
reveal themselves, and sometimes they will not seem
to come at all. As a squirrel has to work hard with a
nut to get the meat out of it, so does a writer with an

idea. No matter how exciting it seemed when it first fused with imagination, it is not always going to be easy to get it out of the mind and down on paper. Like quicksilver, it may seem to divide and run off in quivering drops; like molasses on a cold day, it may seem to have no ability to flow; but it is there and it will respond. Hold the idea before your gaze and wonder about it. Listen to what it has to say. Ask yourself more questions and diligently search for the answers.

How long your story may be only you can tell. A school composition would have to conform to a prescribed length, but because you are writing for yourself you are free to use any length that suits your need. There is a saying that a good story is always the right length, or can be made the right length; but there is a rule that determines this. It is the only rule I know that does, and it is this: Have something to say and stop when you have said it.

How to Start with an Interesting Beginning
and How to Make an Ending Come Gradually

You want to know about beginnings, you want to know about endings. Between these two lies the story. They hold it within their clasp like two hands. Between them they determine whether the reader will want to read at all and whether he will be glad that he has read. Each is important. One is invitation. The other is impact.

As a straight line is the shortest distance between two points, so is it between the words of a writer and the heart of a reader. A story demands an immediate beginning. In the first lines, first two or three paragraphs, half-page, the reader's attention is to be won; descriptions of the time and place of the story, or the conflict that is to be resolved, may all be necessary, but they will be rightly met further on. The reader wants to know where he is; what he wants to do is to get into stride as quickly as possible with the characters who make up the story, and start living their lives. You know yourself that when you begin to read a story, it will not seem far removed from your experience—no matter what its setting or period—if the first few lines persuade you to a way of living in which you can share for a while.

Let's think back to the old fairy tales, the ones you listened to long before you knew how to read and the ones that you read to yourself as soon as you could read. Almost without exception, they begin in the same way and they end in the same way. The beginning intrigues, the ending satisfies, and this is as it should be. *Once upon a time*—you read on and discover that you are in a world of kings and queens, of castles perched on mountaintops, of swans that talk, of witches who brew evil spells, and of bold-hearted princes who learn how to break the spells. Anything may happen and everything does. The first few words established the possibility of such lands and people, such situations, and you read eagerly to see what would follow.

These four words—*once upon a time*—may not be used literally by present-day writers, but their sense is in the first few lines of every story that asks to be read. They are the words that locate the action, that lead into introduction of characters, that hint of the plot that is to develop. They are the words that draw the reader in and give him the feeling that he will soon be part of something that he is going to care very much about. Whether he is to be amused or mystified or informed, he will respond with attention if he is gripped by these words. In whatever way you say your *once upon a time*, let those first few words be instant in establishing communication between you and your reader.

It is in the early sentences that the mood of a story is set, its pace determined, and its climate created. Within all this a group of characters will begin to live. If mood, pace, and climate are convincing, whatever the characters do will seem completely acceptable. Much of what is said at the beginning will be in the way of hints and suggestions, but anything so introduced is brought in because it has a purpose to serve and is to aid in developing the general idea. The little nudges given a reader at the start of a story are like so many seeds sown in prepared ground. Each one will grow as the story grows; each one will add its life to the life of the whole. The *once upon a time* is a signpost that tells the reader both where he is and where he may find himself going.

However long or short the old fairly tales were, they ended invariably with the words *and they lived happily ever after*. This is only another way of saying that all that has been introduced and with which the reader has become involved has been brought to conclusion.

The ending may not necessarily be the happy one of the fairy tales, but it can be richly satisfying.

This does not all take place on the last page, or even on the last two or three pages. The end of a story grows out of the beginning and is in direct relation to it. It has been happening all through the story as the seeds sown early grew and matured and were gathered into the harvest. Some may have been gathered sooner than others, but all were counted in. Characters played out their parts; events served their various purposes; conflicts were resolved; the main character solved the most difficult problem and merited a reward. It has been logical within the wide bounds of imagination, not coincidental. There is nothing left to be said by the writer, for a careful ending leaves no unanswered questions; but there is a great deal for the reader to go on thinking about. The tempting taste at the beginning that promised so much has become a full rich savor at the end.

A short story will be contained between the *once upon a time* and the *lived happily ever after*; a book will depend upon a series of chapters each of which may be, in its own way, like a little short story. But because each chapter builds toward the whole, each one makes a link with the one that is to follow. A chapter may deal with an incident, it may develop a character, it may create some special feeling. Whatever its single purpose, the reader should always be aware of its part within the whole. A chapter satisfies in certain aspects; it stimulates curiosity as well. Each one holds a hint of what may happen when the reader turns to the next.

You have been reading books to understand something about their structure. Read now to understand something about their beginnings and endings. Take one book after another from your shelf of favorite books. Read the first few paragraphs and see how quickly they get you into the story. Then forget about the story for a moment, or pretend that you have read it in great gulps, and turn to the last few paragraphs. Read them to see how neatly the events have been brought together, how the words satisfy you and yet leave you with a sense of being wide to wonder.

Look at the first few lines of *Alice's Adventures in Wonderland*:

> Alice was beginning to get very tired of sitting by her sister on the bank, and of having nothing to do: once or twice she had peeped into the book her sister was reading, but it had no pictures or conversations in it, "and what is the use of a book," thought Alice, "without pictures or conversations?"
> So she was considering, in her own mind (as well as she could, for the hot day made her feel very sleepy and stupid), whether the pleasure of making

a daisy-chain would be worth the trouble of getting up and picking the daisies, when suddenly a White Rabbit with pink eyes ran close by her.

What have these first words done but persuade you to believe that it is a drowsy summer day and Alice is on the edge of falling asleep. In a dream anything may happen; anyone may leave the immediate world and even go down a rabbit-hole.

And how does it end?

"Wake up, Alice dear!" said her sister. "Why, what a long sleep you've had!"

"Oh, I've had such a curious dream!" said Alice. And she told her sister, as well as she could remember them, all these strange Adventures of hers that you have just been reading about; and, when she had finished, her sister kissed her, and said, "It *was* a curious dream, dear, certainly; but now run in to your tea: it's getting late." So Alice got up and ran off, thinking while she ran, as well she might, what a wonderful dream it had been.

Fun as it is to have adventures, it is a good ending that returns us all to something as matter-of-fact as afternoon tea.

Peter Pan begins nimbly, yet within the first four words a sense of mystery has been established:

All children, except one, grow up. They soon know that they will grow up, and the way Wendy knew was this. One day when she was two years old . . .

And at the end, that brief beginning that hinted so much is accounted for in the final paragraph. It is wistful, and very beautiful, and the last words are like another beginning:

. . . and thus it will go on, so long as children are gay and innocent and heartless.

See how *Little Women* begins:

"Christmas won't be Christmas without any presents," grumbled Jo, lying on the rug.

"It's so dreadful to be poor!" sighed Meg, looking down at her old dress.

"I don't think it's fair for some girls to have plenty of pretty things, and other girls nothing at all," added little Amy, with an injured sniff.

"We've got Father and Mother and each other," said Beth contentedly, from her corner.

In four sentences we have met the four characters who will make the story, and we already know something about each one. We understand Jo because she sounds so natural. We sympathize with Meg, are perplexed by Amy, and we heartwarm to Beth. Caring about them all, we are eager to discover what kind of world they live in.

It is a long book. The girls grow up and move out from their home into homes of their own. There are sorrow and joy, accomplishment, disappointment, and all that goes into living. At the end there is deep content, and their adored mother is given the last line in the book:

"O my girls, however long you may live, I never can wish for you a greater happiness than this!"

And now let's open *Charlotte's Web* and read the first page:

"Where's Papa going with that ax?" said Fern to her mother as they were setting the table for breakfast.

"Out to the hog house," replied Mrs. Arable. "Some pigs were born last night."

"I don't see why he needs an ax," continued Fern, who was only eight.

"Well," said her mother, "one of the pigs is a runt. It's very small and weak, and it will never amount to anything. So your father has decided to do away with it."

"Do *away* with it?" shrieked Fern. "You mean *kill* it? Just because it's smaller than the others?"

Mrs. Arable put a pitcher of cream on the table. "Don't yell, Fern!" she said. "Your father is right. The pig would probably die anyway."

Fern pushed a chair out of the way and ran outdoors. The grass was wet and the earth smelled of springtime. Fern's sneakers were sopping by the time she caught up with her father.

How much we know from that first page! The story will be on a farm, and we have already met a determined little girl and her practical parents. Without a doubt, the runt of the litter will be a major character. He is, of course, and his name is Wilbur, but when Charlotte, the spider, swings onto the scene, she too .is very important.

The ending is so warm and real:

Life in the barn was very good—night and day, winter and summer, spring and fall, dull days and bright days. It was the best place to be, thought Wilbur, this warm delicious cellar, with the garrulous geese, the changing seasons, the heat of the sun, the passage of swallows, the nearness of rats, the sameness of sheep, the love of spiders, the smell of manure, and the glory of everything.

Wilbur never forgot Charlotte. Although he loved her children and grandchildren dearly, none of the new spiders ever quite took her place in his heart. She was in a class by herself. It is not often that someone comes along who is a true friend and a good writer. Charlotte was both.

Are you satisfied with that ending?

Beneath the visible words of these four books, can you see the invisible *once upon a time* and *lived happily ever after?* They are there. They are what led you into reading each book and what rewarded you at the end. Whether it was ordinary experience like *Little Women*, or extraordinary like *Peter Pan*, or a blend of both like *Charlotte's Web*, didn't you find that you gave yourself to it because of something in the beginning that won not only your attention but also your heart? Living in the book as long as it lasted, did you not find that you returned to your own world richer by the new friends you had made and the understanding you had gained?

How to Continue—but Not too Far—
and Keep Your Reader Interested

This depends largely on plot and characterization.

The plot is the reason for the story. It is a series of episodes woven back and forth with the central idea gradually being developed through them. It is the basic underlying truth. It is the thread that holds the fabric together. It is what makes the reader want to read on.

It is, as well, a complicated piece of mechanism, though the more skilled a writer becomes in the use of his many tools, the less a plot appears to be contrived and the more completely natural it seems, as if these things must have happened in just this way. But a plot is as necessary to a story as is boiling water for the making of tea.

Stated simply it is this: A story introduces a situation that involves a problem. How does the main character react to the situation and what does he do about the problem? The *what* is the plot. A string of episodes based on convincing adventures cannot be made into a tightly knit story without a plot. A well-written experience with authentic background and carefully drawn characters will become a real story only as it involves a plot—problem stated and subsequently resolved.

Sometimes the plot appears to the reader to depend entirely on the characters and the interest created in them. Events do not seem to matter so much as people and how they respond to all that is happening around them. Sometimes a plot seems difficult to find. If this happens to you, start thinking about a character—how a certain person will feel when confronted with a challenge and what action might logically be pursued; then go on to discover how a second situation arising out of the first might be met. Often, when doing that, the plot that has seemed so elusive will begin to appear.

Some writers, in their approach to a story, will work out the plot carefully from beginning to end before ever they commence to write; others will get to know their characters so well that what the characters do is what only they could possibly do in given situations. That means far more than acquaintanceship with the characters; it means living with them, letting them grow in imagination, loving them as a parent does a child and giving them what they need for their development, then letting them lead their own lives.

A writer may become too indulgent with his characters, or he may expect too much from them; but if they are to be real people, and not dummies to be moved around at his inclination, he will have to understand them. Only as he knows why they do what they do and why they say what they say will the reader have a feeling that he knows why, too. A writer can never take it for granted that a reader knows what he knows. Throughout, the reader must be shown; but there are times when this is as effectively done by what is not said as by what is said.

As an artist does with lines in a sketchbook, draw your characters with words in your notebook. Draw them in the round so that to you they live and breathe. Have a sense of their backgrounds, of the sort of houses they live in, of the details of living that surround them, even of the friends they are capable of making. They are nearer to you than any neighbors. Soon they will seem no longer imaginary but completely real. Give them names and describe them, even to the clothes they wear, their ways of speech and little mannerisms that make them distinctive. Get to know them so well that you would recognize any of them if you met on the street. No one of them will ever be all good or all bad; each one will have shadings that will indicate his or her humanity.

Love them and listen to them. The likelihood is

that they will begin to tell you their different stories. That is what you will write down, adapting what they have to say into what you want to say. At times you may find it necessary to stop yourself and ask, "Am I saying this or is my character?" You may have to wait for the character to catch up with you and say the words in his way.

One of the characters will be, for a reason perhaps only you will ever know, a little closer to you than the others. You will have more sympathy for his views, more concern about his welfare. This will be your main character, and as you tend to identify yourself with him, so will your reader. It is your privilege, as the writer, to have an omnipresent view. With this, you may easily move in and out of the thoughts of your various characters; but one will be in a little sharper focus, and you should maintain that throughout the story. Your long acquaintance will serve you well here, and your growing skill. It will not move your reader greatly to tell him that your character is honest, but if you can show him doing something that is clearly honest, you will have put your point over and the reader will feel as if he had made the discovery for himself. You, as the writer, are simply producing all the evidence that you can, leaving it to the reader to form his own opinion.

You ask me how a writer finds characters, and my

answer is similar to that for subjects. They are all around us, many of them rich and rare and forceful but not fully realized because our attention has not been aroused. Observe the people who make up your world. Be more and more sensitively aware of them. See them as they are, not as you think they ought to be. Wonder about them, for in that process you will begin to understand why they do certain things. Listen to the way they talk, and try to catch beneath the words what it is they are really trying to say.

Then, when you come to create a fictional character, you will have a basis in fact; all the rest will be supplied from the deep well within you that renews itself the more it is drawn on—your imagination. The characters who gain their momentum across your pages will be composed of many elements drawn from many sources; convincing types they will be, but in no wise recognizable as known individuals.

During your apprenticeship you will find more leeway for your thoughts if you write in the third person, especially when you are constructing a piece of fiction. The first person has many limitations, not the least of them being the tangle you run into when you try to describe yourself on paper. Often a story written in the first person does not challenge the reader to participation because—oddly enough—the constant "I" gets in the way. The first person can be intimate and direct, as it is now in the way I am writing to you, but you will find that the third person gives greater range.

Balance your observation of human nature with that of nature. The wide universe of space is not so important to you as the dear, near world where a robin sings from a blossoming tree, a butterfly hovers over a flower, a cricket chirps, a snowflake lies against the window glass for a moment of startling beauty, and then vanishes.

Watch what is going on around you, curiously and yet courteously too. Listen to a squirrel's voluble chatter. Follow the course of a leaf as it drifts with the wind. See how sunlight glances off the hills or off a tall building. Jot down in your notebook what these impressions do to you, and use words that have precision in their syllables. Wherever you live, you can never be far from nature in some of its forms. Your response in one instance will stimulate your ability to keep responding, and what you capture in your notebook may have many uses. Difficult as it is to believe, there are some people who walk through life and fail to see many things, who miss many sounds, who cannot imagine what it might be like to be a swallow swirling through the morning sky; but you can be the sort of person on whom no thing of beauty or whisper of wonder is lost.

Look at everything around you as if you shared its

secret life. Listen and let the thing itself tell you its story. John Burroughs wrote: "My thoughts go and scratch with the hens, they nip the new grass with the geese, they follow the wild ducks northward." The intensity of your imagination will have much to do with the vivid quality and the spacious breadth of your writing. You are the eyes of your reader; you are the ears; you may often be the heart. As you see and hear and feel, so will your reader.

Before we began to write this chapter, you asked me how the story could be continued "but not too far." In other words, you do not want to weary your reader or lose his attention before the problem that has been stated or implied has been satisfactorily resolved. Within that interlocking organization of plot and character, there will be many areas of conversation and many passages of description. The first will do much to enliven your subject matter; the second will do much to enrich it. Together they contribute to the flow of the story and to its development. Let's take them up separately.

Conversation

An exchange of words between characters gives ease and rapidity to reading. The words should be reasonable, persuasive, and completely natural. The interchange may be brisk or loquacious, as long as it is in character, but people should not talk for the mere sake of talking. Whatever is said, in many words or few, must have bearing on the story, either in development of the general idea or in delineation of the characters involved. Conversation does much to endear characters to a reader; it can convey much humor and a great deal of action. It should happen as it does when we hear it or take part in it, that is, without unnecessary identification. If you make it clear who is speaking and who is replying, you will not have to clutter your page with frequent repetitions of "he said" and "she said."

Listen to conversation as you hear it around you, and notice how a certain manner of speaking and use of words will distinguish one person from another. Ponder it in the books you read and see how much it does to increase your feeling for the characters as well as to move you along with the story. In *Charlotte's Web* there is a great deal of conversation. The animals talk to one another in their world, the human beings to one another in theirs, but the boundary is maintained between the worlds, and never crossed except in signs or noises that can be mutually understood. Wilbur the pig, who is in constant danger of becoming bacon, has many long conversations with Charlotte, the spider, who is working on a plan to save him. Listen to them as they talk together, and note how essential is every word:

"When do you work on it?" begged Wilbur.

"When I'm hanging head-down at the top of my web. That's when I do my thinking, because then all the blood is in my head."

"I'd be only too glad to help in any way I can."

"Oh, I'll work it out alone," said Charlotte. "I can think better if I think alone."

"All right," said Wilbur. "But don't fail to let me know if there's anything I can do to help, no matter how slight."

"Well," replied Charlotte, "you must try to build yourself up. I want you to get plenty of sleep, and stop worrying. Never hurry and never worry! Chew your food thoroughly and eat every bit of it, except you must leave just enough for Templeton. Gain weight and stay well—that's the way you can help. Keep fit, and don't lose your nerve. Do you think you understand?"

"Yes, I understand," said Wilbur.

"Go along to bed, then," said Charlotte. "Sleep is important."

Wilbur trotted over to the darkest corner of his pen and threw himself down. He closed his eyes. In another minute he spoke.

"Charlotte?" he said.

"Yes, Wilbur?"

"May I go out to my trough and see if I left any

of my supper? I think I left just a tiny bit of mashed potato."

"Very well," said Charlotte. "But I want you in bed again without delay."

Wilbur started to race out to his yard.

"Slowly, slowly!" said Charlotte. "Never hurry and never worry!"

And so it goes on until the last good nights are said. If a spider and pig could talk together, they would probably sound like Charlotte and Wilbur, and that is as conversation should be.

Description

Description, too, advances the story. It gives the reader a clear image and a more intense feeling of being within the action. Whether a description be of a person, a sunrise, a room, or a meal, it should relate to the whole and have a definite bearing on the developing idea. A story moves in a straight line from beginning to end, and a reader's attention moves with it. Anything injected because it appeals to the writer's delight in words and is not necessary to the story itself will be detected by the reader. A small amount of attention is lost, and the clock, rather than the next page, may begin to draw the eye of the reader.

However, descriptions, no matter how detailed, if

closely related to the developing idea will hold the reader as something he must be familiar with for full appreciation of the story. Skip he may if he dares, but go back he certainly will, for he will find something incomplete in his own thinking later on. In *Little Women*, look at that single paragraph of description that comes in the course of the first few pages:

> Margaret, the eldest of the four, was sixteen, and very pretty, being plump and fair, with large eyes, plenty of soft, brown hair, a sweet mouth, and white hands, of which she was rather vain. Fifteen-year-old Jo was very tall, thin, and brown, and reminded one of a colt; for she never seemed to know what to do with her long limbs, which were very much in her way. She had a decided mouth, a comical nose, and sharp, gray eyes, which appeared to see everything, and were by turns fierce, funny, or thoughtful. Her long, thick hair was her one beauty; but it was usually bundled into a net, to be out of her way. Round shoulders had Jo, big hands and feet, a flyaway look to her clothes, and the uncomfortable appearance of a girl who was rapidly shooting up into a woman, and didn't like it. Elizabeth—or Beth, as everyone called her—was a rosy, smooth-haired, bright-eyed girl of thirteen, with a shy manner, a timid voice, and a peaceful expression, which was seldom disturbed. Her father called her "Little Tranquillity," and the name suited her excellently; for she seemed to live in a happy world

of her own, only venturing out to meet the few whom she trusted and loved. Amy, though the youngest, was a most important person—in her own opinion at least. A regular snow maiden, with blue eyes, and yellow hair curling on her shoulders, pale and slender, and always carrying herself like a young lady mindful of her manners. What the characters of the four sisters were we will leave to be found out.

That is a fairly solid descriptive paragraph, but could you have skipped a single word?

It is relatively easy to write about something; it is more difficult to write the thing itself, and to do so calls for the keenest observation on the part of the writer. Train yourself to accurate observation. Compel your eyes *really* to see how rain looks when it is falling, and your ears *really* to hear how a fire engine sounds as it answers an alarm. What does a cat's fur *really* feel like? And that apple you bit into, what did it *really* taste like? And the smell of woodsmoke rising from a campfire, is there a word that will *really* describe it? This is your challenge. The correct word will be the effective one, and it may never have been used before in just the way you decide to use it.

Strong, clear words are within your grasp; vivid words, full of flavor and honest emotion; words in harmony with your subject matter and appealing to the particular readers you have in mind. Seek out those words, then gain facility in usin g them. Mark Twain said: "The difference between the right word and the almost right word is the difference between the lightning and the lightning bug."

Remember the Beatrix Potter books that you "read" when you were little? Their use of words is a lesson for any writer. In the *Tale of Tom Kitten,* Mrs. Tabitha Twitchett dresses her children in their party clothes, for she is expecting friends to tea. The kittens are told to keep themselves tidy, but they romp and play and their clothes suffer. Then their mother discovers them sitting on the garden wall with no clothes on.

> "My friends will arrive in a minute, and you are not fit to be seen; I am affronted," said Mrs. Tabitha Twitchett.

Does it matter that a three- or four-year-old has not heard the word "affronted" before? It is the right word in the right place, and it will, no doubt, become a permanent part of his vocabulary.

Graphic writing—words that create pictures in the reader's mind—never requires illustrations. They may be added as a happy kind of complement, but no picture should be depended on to take the place of words.

Descriptions, with a visual quality of their own, create a world so real that the reader lives in it. It may be a world of fact or fantasy; it may belong to the past, the present, or even the future; but for the length of the story it is the only world.

There is still another approach to the question of "how to continue but not too far," and that is the extent to which you can satisfy your reader. Assuming that your story is distinctly worth telling, it should leave the reader with a feeling that he has gained something—adventure, fun, experience, a new insight, a fresh outlook; but he should not feel as if he had gained too much. Something should be left for his imagination to feed on, his curiosity to work over. You wondered, and your wondering expanded into a story; now let the reader complete what you commenced as he goes on with the ideas that you have given him.

The style with which you write will do more than anything else to win your reader and to hold his attention, and style is something that you will continue to develop every day of your writing life. Style is mysterious and yet completely obvious. It is *you*. The way you wear your clothes is your style, or lack of it; so is the way you walk down a street. Dash, authority, poise, warmth, grace—all are involved in style. Style is not something arrived at soon and then employed; it is something constantly growing, evolving, changing, and the influences that affect your life affect your style. The way you write now is not the way you will write ten years from now, or twenty, or thirty; but if you write with care and faith, your writing will be distinctly you now, as it will be twenty years from now.

See clearly and write what you see. Feel deeply and write what you feel. Eyes, heart, mind, hand unite to give you your interpretation of the world in which you are a part. This is the essential you, quite different from anyone else and quite capable of doing things in your own way. An apprentice learns the skills of the trade so that when he becomes a master craftsman he may be his own best self.

Be aware of style in the books you read. Often a style is so distinct and recognizable that there is no need to turn to the title page: the words of themselves proclaim who wrote them. Perhaps you never thought of this as style, but you sensed a quality in the writing that held you. Beatrix Potter said that when she felt her style needed chastening, she opened her Bible and read in it for a while. You, too, will find ways to strengthen and invigorate your style as you develop it.

When you have thought long about a story idea and gone deeply into your self for answers to the questions that teased your mind, words will begin to come to you with which you can express your idea.

The words will take on a cadence pleasing to your ear. You will fit them into the construction of sentences with a certain rhythm that is all your own. Only you can decide just how you will do this, but the way in which you do it is your style.

This takes time; it takes caring; it takes constant practice. Don't be too concerned now about your style. Yours will grow as you grow.

4

Something About a Story That Is True

WE have been talking about stories that are made up —fiction; now we are going to talk about something quite different—biography. This will be true to life, or as true to life as it can be made with the facts at hand and the information that can be acquired. You will begin to learn the mastery of a new tool called research. You will begin to accept a new discipline known as vision.

In writing biography you have a responsibility to fact. You are setting yourself to portray the life of a person who really lived. You will have to try to see that person as nearly as possible as he was in his own period of time. You will have to understand something about the hope that motivated him, to learn how it was that he left his mark on time. This requires vision, and though vision is related to the observation we have been talking about, it is far more penetrating. To discover something, even if it be only a hint, of the dream by which a man lives is an important part of the search that precedes the writing of a biography.

Vision may be your discipline, but research will be your tool and you will have to learn to handle it well. If you want to write about a historical character, you will have to read much that has already been written about that person and about the period in which he lived. A story based on actual life must be correct in known details. As you begin to draw facts from many sources, a new kind of notebook work will be necessary. You may decide to list your findings chronologically under the years; you may decide to list them episodically under significant events. However you list them, keep careful record of the sources from which you drew your information. You may need to go back to them to refresh your own memory; you may need to prove to some questioner the existence of your reference material.

If the background is to be that of another country, you will have to make a mental journey there by means of an atlas, a geography, a travel book, and probably a brief history, so you will know the locale well enough to have a working knowledge about it. You may have to check your findings from time to time with other sources of information.

If you are writing about animal lives, you will want to search the rich store of material written by natural-ists, biologists, and such people for the real behavior and actual habits of animals that are known to competent observers.

As you read, try to get below the surface of your research and discover what will be meaningful for the present-day reader. There is a rule about research, and it is this: Know when to stop. A good idea for a story can sometimes get bogged down, even lost forever, in too lengthy research. Read widely and pursue all the clues you can find; then spend fully as much time thinking about what you have read. Let your reading become a part of you, and begin to write only when you can clothe your garnered facts in your own words. You may use no more than a small portion of all that you have learned, but your research has created an actual world in which you can live. Much of the flavor and sense of place in your writing will come from your background reading.

You ask about a story that is partly true and partly made up, like that of a young person (imagined) in a Civil War setting (fact). The first part will be up to you to handle in the fictional manner that is most appealing to you; the second part relies on research, and will make your words credible. There are many ways to supplement the knowledge gained in history books. A file of newspapers for the 1860's in the public library will set a tone for the then contemporary life. There will be some pictures that will give an idea of how people looked and an indication of the way they lived. There will be advertisements describing the things they used—household furnishings, food, clothes. Social items will tell of how they entertained themselves. Even the proper names have the ring of another time, and the manner of address is different from that of the present.

A few touches in a story, based on authentic research, will establish a reader quickly and comfortably in another period. There is much, of course, that you will never be able to find out about the way of living in other days. Use well what you can, and what is meaningful, but don't feel that you have to use everything. Your story will speak more convincingly to the reader if it is free of creaking reminders of research.

An incident that I heard of has a bearing on biographical writing. One day a horse got out of his pasture, and the farmer went in search of him but could not find the horse anywhere. His neighbors came to help him in the search, but it was all to no avail. When the farmer's son returned from school, his mother told him about the missing horse, and said, "Now, son, you go out and look too." He did, and soon returned leading the horse. Asked where and how he had found him so quickly, the boy replied: "It was easy. I figured to myself if I were a horse where would I go. I did and he had."

It is the same for the person who chooses a biographical subject. He will have to imagine himself to be his subject; he will have to think himself into another person and see things through other eyes. He will do it better if there is something that speaks to him from within the subject in a language his heart can understand.

Imagine that you stand face to face across the span of a hundred years with an actual person about whom you want to write a story. The life that was filled with service and achievement has now become part of history, but during the living of it wasn't it like any life? It must have held obstacles and problems, sorrow and disappointments. The more obstacles there were, and the more gallantly they were surmounted, the more effective the life became. What were the particular problems? How were they faced and overcome? Why was this done? What lessons were learned? And what was the result? There is good reason why that particular life continues to shine, but what is the reason?

Again it is a ceaseless asking of questions, but you have much to aid you in arriving at the answers. There may be published letters. There will be written lives, or at least biographical sketches in encyclopedias. There may even be people to talk with who can give you helpful information. But no matter what exists already, you will still have to formulate your own answers to the questions that rise in your mind.

This kind of thinking calls for patience on your part and a hand as steady as that of a miner when he follows the vein that leads to the mother lode. It is long and slow and wearying, though it has its moments of excitement, this journey back into another period of time, this penetration into another way of thinking; but at some point during the journey the actual person you are seeking may seem to come to meet you. Now the miles that have stood between you will mean no more than the years, and you may feel—almost—as if you had clasped hands with your chosen subject. This is the moment when the dream by which another lived becomes clear to you.

"But I have felt that way too!" you want to exclaim.

True biography creates a oneness of outlook, a feeling that in the essentials people are very much the same.

How can you take this sudden, brilliant recognition of the significance of another's life and incorporate it with the historical facts and daily details that you have been learning? You will do it by the imaginative use of your writer's tools, as an artist uses his imaginatively when painting a portrait. Study portraits in galleries or art books, and notice how the artist ar-

ranges his composition so the eye of the viewer will
be drawn to the face. He may introduce into his
background descriptive items that relate to the work
or position in the world of his subject; or he may
leave his background quite free, and depend on color
harmony, careful placing of hands and other elements
to convey character. Whatever it is, his arrangement
is such that the face, the eyes, the expression compel
attention. A biography in words is like one on canvas.
Its intent is to draw attention to those aspects of the
person that speak for themselves.

Let me tell you about two books of mine that are
based on the lives of actual people—*Amos Fortune,
Free Man* and *Prudence Crandall, Woman of Courage*. With the first, imagination in large measure had
to be used to fill in the spaces in the known material;
with the second, there was a mass of existing material that called for imagination in its presentation.
Each person made a distinct appeal to me. Each
lived by a dream. They were dreams in which I, too,
could share.

What did life do to this man? What did he do to
life? Those were the questions that I asked myself as
I stood beside the grave of Amos Fortune in a New
England churchyard on a summer evening. I read the
brief, but telling, epitaph over and over—"Sacred to
the memory of Amos Fortune who was born free in

Africa, a slave in America, he purchased liberty, professed Christianity, lived reputably and died hopefully. November 17, 1801. Aet. 91." It said much, yet there was so much more that I wanted to know. My mind filled with questions. How was it that he became a slave? When did he purchase his own freedom? What gave him his reputation? And what was the hope by which he lived?

To find the answers I began a search through town records, histories, documents, books on the slave trade. Slowly I worked my way back through the years, following each clue that presented itself, gradually amassing a mound of information. Out of it there began to emerge the story of a single African who had been brought to America at the time when some quarter-million Africans were imported to answer the growing demand for labor. He had been given the name of Amos on the auction block. Later he acquired the name of Fortune. Why?

History was a road that I traveled as far as it would take me; then I came to a point where there was only one signpost, and it was marked *Imagination*. It was a perilous point, but I remembered that Keats in a letter to a friend had once said: "I am certain of nothing but of the holiness of the heart's affection and the truth of Imagination. What the Imagination seizes as beauty must be Truth." Wondering about those words, I came to the conclusion that *if* one was imbued with a subject and immersed in a period, perhaps Imagination could be trusted as a guide. During the writing of Amos Fortune's story, certain things became very clear to me and I set them down; later on, as more information was discovered, those very things were found to be correct.

The house that Amos Fortune built with his own hands and when he was no longer young still stands in Jaffrey, New Hampshire, stalwart and sound, lived in by working people. His lantern has survived, his compass, and many of his precious papers, in particular his freedom paper and his will. Monadnock Mountain, which he gazed at often and whose slopes he knew, looks down on the countryside. All of them helped in the fitting together of the story, as did the recollections given me by descendants of Amos' friends and neighbors.

Amos Fortune would have been the last person to guess that a century and a half after his death his name would still be remembered, but time, events, and human needs sometimes have more to do with the determination of a man's greatness than his immediate contribution. He took a strong stand for individual freedom. The dream that led him, born in his heart and shaped with his life's work, was a dream of freedom based on social responsibility. He knew something about and grounded his life on the inalienable rights all men have through birth. A country churchyard proved to be far too small to hold within it the spirit of Amos Fortune, since all that he stood for in his day is vital in ours.

With *Prudence Crandall, Woman of Courage* there was little need to imagine any of the events that might have taken place in her life. A great deal of material to read and ponder was easily obtainable. State, county, and town histories all told of her. There were accounts in newspapers of the day, records of the three trials in which she figured, and lives of important people who mentioned her in their letters. The town in which she lived for a while and where she taught her school, Canterbury, Connecticut, looks much as it must have looked at her time. Her house is there, and the church. Many of the tall elms must have been young trees when she walked with her scholars beside them.

The story of her seventeen months' endeavor to teach white and Negro girls in the same school is a story of failure, but though she had to bow to failure she did not accept defeat. The basic concept of equality was to her a moral principle, and nothing could force her to relinquish it. For more than fifty years, and long after she had moved to the Midwest, she was listed as a criminal on the books of the State of Connecticut, though after her third trial, conviction had been set aside on a technicality. In 1886 the State Legislature rescinded the action of an early court and granted her a pension, "by way of compensation for injuries done to her person and property by citizens of the town of Canterbury during the years 1833 and 1834." Prudence Crandall Philleo was an old lady then, living on the Kansas plains. She was still teaching, she was still valiant, and she had kept herself free from bitterness. The Civil War had been fought, schools for Negroes had been opened, and colleges were being established. Though she had failed at an earlier time, the cause that was the dream that led her had not been thwarted.

Her life was a long one, spanning a great part of the nineteenth century, but the years in Canterbury were the most dramatic. It was those years of which I wrote. Even with all the material at hand about her, I still had to find my answers to the questions that were in my mind: What had enabled her to be so firm in the face of danger and humiliation? Why did she bend, so soon after her marriage, to her husband's insistence that she close the school? Did marriage put her to the test of obedience? Had she begun to see that there are times when success can come only after apparent failure?

Search as I might, I could discover no living relatives of either Prudence Crandall or Calvin Philleo;

but the book did, after it was published. Prudence's great-niece, a spirited lady well into her nineties and living on the West Coast, wrote to me and said: "For me, Great-aunt lives again."

What a man lives by is what keeps him living on. The thread of gold in another life is the dream that led to fulfillment in that life. It may be clear in written words or remembered conversations. It may be discovered only after research and vision have been faithfully brought to the task, but it is there and it will reveal itself in time. Once you have found it, keep your finger on that golden thread to guide you safely to the end.

And Now—to Write!

To think about a possible story is to set up an inner magnetic field that draws to itself all sorts of ideas, many of them expected and some quite unexpected. You must have found this happening to you while you were thinking about your story and ideas came to you from various sources. Now your notebook is filled with jottings to reinforce you. Your mind is brimming. New discoveries about people have come to you; new appreciation of values is yours. You want to communicate all this to others and you begin to sense that the time to put thoughts into words has come. There is always a moment when the inner time clock strikes and tells you to write.

So, find your quiet place where the blank pages on the pad are waiting and the pencils are sharp. You know what you want to do, and you are, as well, willing to let the idea show you what it must do as it gathers force. A writer is a creator, making new worlds from the materials at hand, and the time of creation is mysterious and wonderful.

Write. Write in the full flow of the inspiration that has taken hold of you. Don't stop to find the exact word or to correct the construction of a sentence; don't worry yourself over a point of grammar. If in need of a word, leave a space, and when you read your work back to yourself later on you may find that the word comes to you then; but if it doesn't, you can take all the time you need to seek it out. The intensity that is yours when you first begin to write may not last too long, so use it well and to the full. Say what you have to say, say what you have been wanting to say; and if the story begins to take a different direction and seems to write itself in a new way, go along with it.

A short piece may be brought to completion at one time of writing; a longer piece may require much more of you. If it does, don't write yourself out completely at one time. Leave a little water to prime the pump. Then when you return to your work, there will be something ready and waiting to be said and you will be able to get going. Before you start, read over a few paragraphs of the work already done, not the whole story but just enough to get you into the swing. Your goal is the completion of this particular story; it is also to do a good and true piece of work. Whether any eyes other than your own will ever see the pages that your hand is racing over will depend on how pleased *you* are with them when the work is finished.

When it is, put it aside for a few days. The most exacting task for a writer is ahead, and that task is revision of the work. You will approach it more readily if the work is given a chance to acquire some objectivity, and time will aid in this. You caught the idea in the fervor of creation. Words came from you in a fast, full flow. You indulged yourself with their abundance. Now you will have to be hard on yourself as you test those very words against the standard you have set for yourself, a standard arrived at through your reading of good literature and your own instinct for writing. The arduous work of revision that is before you will make demands on the sharpness of your eye and the keenness of your ear. It may take more time than the first writing, but it can be as exciting as the creative act, if not more so, and it is what will make of the apprentice a true craftsman.

This is my standard, given to me by an English teacher when I was in school:

> The written word should be
> Clean as a bone,
> Clear as light,
> Firm as stone;
> Two words are not so good
> As one.

Read your work back to yourself, preferably aloud. Hearing will come to the aid of sight to catch delicate gradations· in meaning. The cadence of words, the rhythm in lines, will be more apparent as you listen for the sound. Stop often and ask yourself: "Is this what I really meant to say?" If a word or a phrase or a paragraph is not meaningful to you, it will not be to anyone, so be stern with yourself and follow the well-tried advice "When in doubt, cut it out." Watch and listen for repetitions. Weed them out and weed out any unnecessary words or phrases. Keep your writing lean, muscular, strong, and seek always for a fresh and vigorous use of words.

Be wary of any word or group of words that comes too easily. Cut them out and try using another approach. If you find yourself constantly falling back on adverbs such as *so, very, somehow,* and adverbial phrases like *as a matter of fact,* take a colored pencil and draw a ring around the words wherever they appear on your pages. See how often you use them, and ask yourself what would happen to your writing if you eliminated some of them.

Be alert to a careless reliance on adjectives, using three to describe a noun when one aptly chosen would do as well. And yet, it is your eye and your ear and the sensitive balance within you that must make the final decision. There might be an occasion when three adjectives were demanded and each one would serve a distinct and eloquent purpose.

Check yourself for vague phrases that do not make place, time, or person clear to the reader; and check yourself on the words and phrases that are meaningful only within a particular family or a certain locale. If they are explained and used with definite reason, then that is your writer's privilege. Slang will date a story, so use it if you must, but remember that it has definite limitations.

Tighten wherever you can and take out whatever is not essential to the meaning. Are the first few paragraphs necessary to the story or were they just necessary to you to launch you into the story? Perhaps the story really got into its stride on the second page, and the first can be discarded. Is the end neat and explicit, accounting for the major ideas that were introduced at the beginning and bringing them to conclusion? Is it clear that the problem you began with has been solved? Will the reader feel satisfied? Or is the ending dragged out, labored, perhaps even wearied by anticlimax? As you read it aloud to yourself, you may see suddenly and quite clearly that the ending really came a whole page sooner than when you wrote *Finis*. Resaying something that had already been stated weakened the impact. So, discard the last page.

Perhaps you could make changes indefinitely, just

as you could have gone on gathering ideas indefinitely, but again the inner time clock has a way of striking. A moment comes during the revision when you read your pages through for what you know is the last time and you say to yourself: "That's that." This is the best that you could do, though that is not to say that you may not soon do something else far better. This is what you wanted to say. It does not seem to you now that there is anything you can add to it, nor does it seem that there is anything you can take away from it. It pleases you.

It would be strange if you did not feel, at this particular moment, written out. You may even wonder if words will ever come to you again. You may even begin to have moments of doubt as to whether what you did is any good at all. Doubt can be a saving grace, and when it yields it often leaves more room than ever before for faith. Words will come again. The well within you will be renewed from those never-failing springs that have their rise in your imagination. It is right that now, for a little while, you should have a quiet time. A creative person, it is said, should be a hard worker and a good idler. Before you know it, another idea will be knocking at the door of your mind, and when it does you will find yourself ready to welcome it and eager to question it. It will be new and different, and so will be your approach to it. It will have to prove itself. Growing with it, you will find your skills growing too.

The story that you have written, revised and copied is now ready to be read by someone. You *want* it to be read. So you give it to a friend, a member of your family, perhaps even to your English teacher. If your reader's response is an appreciative "Well done," the words will be music to your ears; but it may not be. The longed-for words of approval may not be uttered, and you must train yourself now not to require them. You did the best piece of work that you could do at the time: that is your confidence and your reward. Another's commendation is not essential to you now, or at any time in your writing career. It can be very pleasant; often it is entirely warranted; but it can spoil you, too.

What if your reader does not like your story— laughs in the wrong places? misses the point? fails to see anything in the character that meant so much to you? This is hard, but it is something a writer meets often, and it is sensible to get used to it. You cannot possibly please everyone, but if you please yourself you have gone a long way. And you are, whether you realize this or not, the hardest person to please. You have set high standards for yourself and you will raise them constantly.

To be a writer you know that you must have something to say. You know, too, that you must have the capacity to work hard and alone and that you must develop a keen sense of self-criticism. When the work is done and has gone out into the world, you must let it go with full faith in it. You cannot afford to be sensitive to opinion. If you are now, you must begin to toughen yourself.

In my story of Dorothy Canfield Fisher, *Pebble in a Pool*, I tell of the time when, as a young girl, she learned to box. Her father was at that time, 1891, Chancellor of the University of Nebraska, and a great educator:

> [He] felt strongly that many of the troubles women experienced throughout their lives resulted from their being too protected. "Criticism, for instance," he said. "Most women take it so personally, Dolly, that they can't profit from it. Some rugged treatment now and then, even getting hit, can help."
>
> "Criticism." Dolly repeated the word, holding it off at arm's length so she could observe it.
>
> "I don't know what you will do with your life, but whatever it is you can't escape criticism," her father went on. "You can make it serve you if you learn how to appraise it and rebound from it."
>
> So Dolly with a group of her friends had boxing lessons. They learned how to use their gloved fists in defense and attack; how to overcome the mis-

takes that took them off guard; how to keep their tempers under control.

Be willing to learn from criticism, no matter how harsh it may be. Be willing to examine your work in the light of honest opinion, and see how you can improve it. You are in the process of growing, and you will continue to grow through every kind of experience as a garden grows through sun and rain and needs both to thrive.

There may be times when you will need to discuss an idea with someone to help you see it clearly, but learn where and from whom you can seek advice. It is good practice not to talk about an idea until you are sure of it yourself, and then only to someone you can trust. It seems so easy for people to be negative; it takes caring and real perception to be affirmative, and the one who can offer the most constructive criticism is the one who has the heart to help. You know your true friend. It is the person who holds you to the best of which you are capable and who enables you to believe in your self.

"Great art," John Masefield says, "does not proceed from great criticism, but from great encouragement."

THE best of all disciplines is to love what you are doing. It then becomes easy to accept necessary restrictions and unusual demands. This is as true for writing as it is for art, music, or any achievement. You will have to keep yourself in training, and the constant exercise of your craft is the way. You should in time, and as your skills develop, obtain the mastery that will enable you to write *if need be* at any moment, in any place, on any subject.

Keep a firm hold on your time, for you will need a great deal. Time is not a commodity that is given to us neatly packaged. It is often something that we have to make for ourselves, setting a portion of it aside carefully, taking a few minutes here and a few minutes there, getting up a half-hour earlier or giving up some pleasant diversion. The test of whether you really want to do a thing, or not, is often in whether you can make the time for it, or not. Have you ever heard people say they are going to write when they have time? The days and the years go on, and the time never comes.

Keep flexible. Use a pencil when you write, and sometimes use a pen. Learn how to use a typewriter; then try composing on it to see if you catch your thoughts more quickly. Type what comes into your head, whether it makes immediate sense or not. The words may have a more casual sound, for often the act of typing frees the mind, and thoughts that seemed imprisoned find release.

Use a lapboard to write on instead of a table or a desk, and try writing in a rocking chair or in bed. If you have a favorite place in an apple tree, beside a brook, or in the stillness of the woods, take your pad and pencil with you and write there. Have you ever tried writing when in a bus or on a train? The gentle movement, the sense of enclosure, the rhythmic sound can do lovely things to your words and your sentence structure. Legibility will not matter, as you will be the only one having to read what has been written.

Be able to write anywhere with any kind of equipment. The more you do it, the more adept you will become in creating around you your own area of quiet, and this is all you really need.

Keep yourself fit, as fit as an athlete. You know

enough about the rules of health to do that—sensible food, a right amount of sleep, and plenty of robust exercise outdoors. The body needs to be maintained at a high state of functioning, for writing demands all one's faculties—keen eyes, sharp ears, relaxed and ready muscles. And, if you have built up a reserve of health to draw upon, you will be able to make demands on your body when and if the need arises. For constant clear thinking, the mind must be kept free of destructive emotions. Learn to control anger and dismiss resentment, for such mental states take a toll on the creative impulse.

All your writing time will not be spent in writing stories. Much of it should be spent in ways that will improve your writing ability. You know, probably better than anyone else, where your weaknesses lie; there are several ways by which you can gradually turn them into strengths. Perhaps you need to improve your power of observation so you can write better descriptive passages. Perhaps you need to learn how to make your dialogue more realistic. Perhaps your characters are not sufficiently convincing. Perhaps your use of words needs sharpening, so words will say what you mean them to say. Here are a few specific exercises for you to do. Each one is only a suggestion, and you can work out for yourself many more that will apply to your own needs.

Observation

Look at the tree outside your window, or one that you pass on your way to school. How does it appear to you at different times of the day and on different days? Compel yourself to see it, as it is under various conditions, and then find words that will make another who may not know the tree see it as you do—in sunshine, in rain, in snow, sleet, fog, bare or fully leafed. It is never the same. Search it with the eyes of a bird seeking a nesting site, with the eyes of a boy who likes to climb, with the eyes of a woodsman who knows the value of timber, with the eyes of the man who planted the tree and who now is old while the tree is in its prime. Go all around the tree mentally, and physically too, as you see it from many viewpoints, as well as your own. Write what you see with the different eyes. Be exact, and as economical with your words as if you were writing a telegram.

Do the same thing with the sunset night after night, in fair weather and on days when the change of light is marked only by subtle variations in the deepening dusk. Notice what the long rays of light do as they lengthen and before they diminish, how they rest on distant hills, illumine clouds, flash from the glass panes of windows. Watch the sun going down as a person would for whom the day has held heartache or hardship. Watch it as one would for whom the next day is to hold some joyous event. Night steals over the world, and the darkness means one thing to one person, and quite something else to another.

Take a close look at the living room in your home first thing in the morning; then study it carefully in the evening. Much will be the same, but there will be evidences of how it has been lived in during the day. There will be many silent reminders of the doings it has witnessed. Try to write what took place there, basing your conclusion on the evidence before your senses.

Dialogue

You have just made a new friend, and, though you could describe her well in a paragraph, you are called upon to describe her in conversation. This is not a question-and-answer interview, but a gay and rapid exchange of words with someone who has your interests at heart. The words will be colloquial; there may even be some easy current slang; and you will have to think quickly and write equally so, just as you would if you were talking.

Pretend that you are on the telephone and write down the conversation as it takes place, but in such a way that though only one conversation is set down it will be clear to anyone who reads your words what the person on the other end of the line has been saying.

It is more difficult to make people laugh than to make them cry, but you should be able to do both. Tell a sympathetic listener about some sad happening you have witnessed or perhaps been involved in; then do a similar thing with a ridiculous occasion. This may well be the most trying exercise you can set yourself. You will do it best with few words rather than with many. A sudden stab to the heart can open floodgates of feeling; the touch of a feather on a sensitive area can have rib-tickling results.

Character

Go back as far as you can in memory and meet yourself as a very little child. What made you happy in those days? What made you sad? Perhaps you can recall a sense of fear that seems unreasoning now because you have outgrown it. Some things, no doubt, called forth your temper, and you acted in a way that seems barbaric to you now. Most people made you conscious of your size and your place, but there might have been someone who made you feel big. Even then, when you stood no higher than a table's edge, you caught a sudden glimpse across the top of what you might begin to be. Now, write a biography of yourself, and when you come to an event that had particular significance try to reconstruct it as fully as you can.

All this will help you to understand yourself a little better, and by doing so you will begin to understand others. This is basic for good character building, either in life or in fiction, and is a source of inner strength.

Here is the second part of this exercise: think of someone who is disliked for any of a dozen reasons, because he is dishonest, unkind, or just plain dull. Go back imaginatively in that person's life and see if you can put your finger on what might have happened at some early time to make him act the way he does now. Start to build on paper your own concept of this character. The long view will give you objectivity; from it will stem tolerance; compassion may then take over. The endeavor to understand one actual person will aid you in the creation of your fictional people.

Words

Take any word that comes readily to your mind. It may be a word used all too frequently and therefore one whose present meaning has strayed far from its original. Lovely. Terrific. Fabulous. Square. Those are all such words. Take one of them, or a word that you fall back on to serve a dozen uses. Put it at the top of a list and then beneath it write all the words that you could use instead. The chances are that you will progress in a fairly roundabout manner to the original meaning. Perhaps the word has become so fogged by misuse that you will have to go to the dictionary to straighten it out in your own mind. That's what dictionaries are for, and anything that will aid you to build a rich and pliant vocabulary is good.

This exercise becomes something of a game, and it is one of the few that you can embark on with other people as well as by yourself, for it is controlled. But now here is one that is free-wheeling. Again, take a word—say, "friend." Place it at the top of a list and write under it in the order in which they come to mind all the words suggested by the first and subsequent words. "Friend" may lead to "Ruth"—then "red hair" —"tomboy"—"basketball"—"Nicky"—"school bus"— and before you know it, an idea for a story with a plot all neatly wrapped up in a remembered experience is taking shape in your thoughts.

But, you say, sometimes you just can't get going. This happens to everyone, and it will continue to happen throughout a writing career. There are days when a piece of paper looks appallingly blank. The mind is blocked. The hand is laggard. There is complete and utter inability to entice words from their secret hiding place to exposure on the paper. There is no simple explanation for this and there is no easy way to keep it from happening. All I can say by way of comfort is to repeat that it happens to every writer.

Sometimes doodling down the page will start a trickle. Sometimes looping letters like an exercise in penmanship will loosen the hand; the mind will respond and a thin but steady flow of thoughts into words will result. Sometimes far more vigorous action is required, and the imagination must be given that to which it can respond.

Take a hint from an art class. The teacher places two dots on the chalkboard and asks a student to connect them. There is action in the line that moves from one dot to the other, whether it be straight or wavy, roundly curved or angular. The writer puts on his paper two nouns—any two that come to mind—"boy, dog"; "child, box"; "man, snowblower." Then he looks at them, but he can't look at them for long without something beginning to happen inside him. He wants to connect them, and he does so with a verb. The link between the two, the lifeline, is action; but the verb is in the writer as much as it is on the page, and action is what was needed. Relationship has been established, and from that fertile ground much will grow.

Here is one final exercise to help you develop your

ability to do research—carefully as you must, imaginatively as you will have to if you are to make an interesting story out of some curious piece of information that has come your way. This is such a piece. I read it one day in a newspaper. It was used as a filler. I cut it out because it intrigued me:

> Little Jack Horner was a real boy and lived in the Abbey of Glastonbury during the reign of Henry VIII. The abbot sent the deed to the abbey to the king concealed in a pie, using Jack as the messenger. Instead of delivering the pie, Jack stole the "plum" and claimed ownership of the property.

So, that old nursery rhyme told of a historical incident! If true, there is a possibility here for a fascinating story. But is it true? That is the first question that will have to be answered. If it is answered affirmatively, a host of other questions will follow fast. Your library will hold the answers, but you will have to dig them out, turning first to an encyclopedia, then to a history of England, then to book after book with excitement mounting. You will begin to feel like a beagle on a trail through the woods as you follow the path back to the past.

And this is exactly what disciplined exercise does: limbers you up so your thinking becomes fluent and the work more exciting.

Salute to a Fellow Craftsman

You say that you wish someone would discover a talent in you, but you have done that yourself in your desire to be a writer. You know, now, a litttle more of how a writer works and you have glimpsed something of the manner in which the raw material of everyday experience can be transmuted into the finished fabric of stories. You know, too, that the only way to progress in writing is to write, to do the best you can with each piece of work, sure that you will do better with the next.

Can you remember when you first knew you wanted to write? I doubt it, for I think you were born into the world with the desire. Imagination, a sense of humor, a feeling for drama were born with you, too, but that is not unusual because they are the birthright of most children. You do have, however, two special gifts. One might be called a sense of curiosity that makes you want to find out things for yourself, the other, a sense of courage that enables you to hold to the vision that you see. There is a third, perhaps not a gift but the result of the two gifts working together— confidence in your ability to accomplish the task you set yourself.

Let me illustrate in a brief biography.

Once upon a time a child was born, richly endowed as children are, and capable of doing great good in life. This child seemed to possess a special gift of curiosity. The use of this often required a certain amount of courage; but courage had been a special gift, too, for it was there to be drawn upon. And the two gifts grew as the child grew. In the course of time, curiosity and courage working together aided in the development of self-confidence that began to serve the child worthily. Using natural endowments well and special gifts to the full, the child grew up to be a writer . . . and lived happily ever after.

Between the traditional beginning and ending, a long space of time is involved. In these talks together we have called it your apprenticeship. Nothing can make it any shorter—not eagerness to achieve, not willingness to work hard, not even the intensity of your desire—for it is the way of growth that it is always slow. But when it is accomplished and you stand on the threshold of your writing career, you will be glad that the days of your apprenticeship were as long as they were.

Let your imagination follow the course of a seed in the dark earth. Secretly feeding and growing, it waits until the time is right for it to begin to stretch up to the light. The roots that have been reaching deep reach deeper as the stem strengthens and begins to thrust itself through the soil. Pushing up and up, it grows strong because the roots are strong; it unfolds, blossoms, ripens, and fulfills its function of beauty, of use, of being.

In a similar fashion, you are growing. The process, so like that of nature, makes you one with the great rhythm of life. There is no quick way or easy, but the only way is sure. In nature the days fulfill each other until the seed pushes through the ground and reaches up to the sky to become an oak; the child struggles into the world and starts toward maturity. It is a long, slow process, and nothing has ever been found that can speed it up; but every moment is fraught with significance, for while something is becoming it is being, too.

As you go on during the years of your apprenticeship, you will find many books to read about writing itself. They will tell you of different techniques, of different approaches to this most ancient of crafts, of different methods of work. There will be much that you can learn from them, but you will always be your own best teacher. You will be the one to make the demands on yourself; you will be the one to hold yourself to the high standard. As you reach outward and upward, as you look deeply within, you will gain more knowledge and a wider compassion; you will also learn more about yourself and your relation to the world in which you live.

You have your writer's tools, not so many compared to some crafts, but with them you will shape the vehicle that will carry what you want to say into the minds of others. Tools are as effective as the one who handles them, and it is important to know yourself and to make the most of that self, for what you write about will never be so meaningful as what you are.

Your experience is your own-ness; it is also your one-ness with the rest of mankind. Words are the bridge for the writer. With them one heart reaches to another, one mind is quickened by another, across the span of the centuries or the miles or the little lonelinesses of life. If sometime, someday, someone unknown to you reads your words, shares your vision, and inwardly exclaims, "I have felt that way too!" you will have won your reward.

That is the goal. Keep your thoughts toward it and cherish these years of work that are readying you for its attainment. Carl Sandburg was once asked by a friend, "In all those years when you were working and working, did you ever doubt that you would eventually get there?" He answered without hesitation: "I didn't think about it. There was something I wanted to say."

ELIZABETH YATES was born in Buffalo, New York, and attended The Franklin School there. Summers were spent on her father's farm where she transformed an unused pigeon loft into a secret writing place. She liked to make up stories, especially when riding her horse through the countryside; then, on rainy days, she would go to her pigeon loft and write them out. When school days were over, she went to New York where she worked and studied for three years. At the age of twenty-three she married William McGreal, an American whose business was in England, and for several years they lived in London. The McGreals now live in Peterborough, New Hampshire and Elizabeth's days are divided between writing, gardening, community activities and deep enjoyment of the countryside.

Her first work to be published was a poem in a metropolitan newspaper soon after she left school, but it was not until ten years later that her first book appeared—the culmination of a long apprenticeship in writing. She has written distinguished books for adults, as well as for children, and received many notable awards, among them the Newbery Medal and the William Allen White Children's Book Award for *Amos Fortune, Free Man,* and for other books the Gold Medal of the Boys' Clubs of America and the Annual Award of the Women's International League for Peace and Freedom. For several years she has been conducting workshops at Writers Conferences and more than a score of published writers are numbered among her students.